Copyright © 2009 by Quirk Productions, Inc.

Library of Congress Cataloging in Publication Number: 2008940482

ISBN: 978-1-59474-414-3

Printed in Malaysia

Typeset in Goudy and Monotype Old Style

Designed by Doogie Horner and Jenny Kraemer
Illustrations by Vic Kulihin
Production management by John J. McGurk

The jokes on pages 96 and 97 first appeared in *Jokes Every Man Should Know* by Don Steinberg. Reprinted by permission of the publisher.

Distributed in North America by Chronicle Books
680 Second Street
San Francisco, CA 94107

10 9 8 7 6 5 4 3 2

Quirk Books
215 Church Street
Philadelphia, PA 19106
www.quirkbooks.com

STUFF

Every Man Should Know

by Brett Cohen

QUIRK BOOKS
PHILADELPHIA

To my dad,
for teaching me half of this stuff.

To my wife and family,
for teaching me the rest.

Introduction

Here are a few things that I learned in school:

- How to calculate the circumference of a circle
- How to ask "May I go to the bathroom?" in Spanish
- The hierarchy of leadership in the medieval feudal system

Here are a few things that I did not learn in school:

- How to calculate my golf handicap
- How to pick up a girl in Spanish
- The hierarchy of poker hands

There's a pattern here: School will teach you reading, writing, and everything you need to ace a standardized test. But the classroom will get you only so far—especially if you're a man.

Men should know how to jump-start a car. Men should know how to start a campfire. Men should know how to order wine from a waiter in a five-star restaurant. But if you're like most guys, no one ever told you how to do any of this stuff.

That's where this book comes in. It's a compendium of all the little things guys are expected to know—from doing push-ups and shotgunning a beer to deciphering the *Wall Street Journal* stock index. I've included instructions for stocking a bar, filling a toolbox, and buying a basic wardrobe. Along the way I've included information that's not truly essential but still kind of fun—so the next time you're challenged to shotgun a beer, you'll know exactly what to do.

Now sit back, relax, and pay attention. This stuff is important.

THE
STUFF

How to Build a Campfire

The discovery of fire is one of man's greatest accomplishments. Using these instructions, you should have an easier time than our cavemen counterparts.

1. Clear an area at least 10 feet (roughly 3 meters) in diameter. Be sure there is no low-hanging debris nearby. If a fire pit already exists, be sure that all materials, such as tents, clothes, and blankets, are at least 3 feet (1 meter) away from the fire pit.

2. If a fire pit exists, skip ahead to step 3. If not, place rocks or bricks in a circle that is approximately 3–4 feet (1 meter) in diameter.

3. Gather materials. You will need a mixture of kindling, sticks, and larger logs.

   a. Kindling is light-weight material that will burn quickly and get the fire started. This could be a mixture of twigs, paper, dry leaves, and/or dry pine needles.

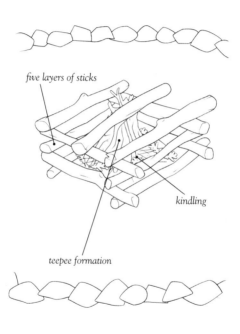

five layers of sticks

kindling

teepee formation

✦ The Log-Cabin Fire ✦

b. Sticks should be a little bulkier and broken to fit inside the fire pit. The sticks should be dead and dry.

c. Larger logs should be dry and able to fit safely inside the fire pit.

4. Place a few handfuls of kindling in the center of the fire pit.

5. Stack the sticks around the kindling in a teepee form. The sticks should lie at a 45 degree angle from the ground, and you should leave room between the sticks to allow oxygen to flow through the teepee.

6. Using the thicker sticks, create a square around the teepee structure. You can do this by placing two sticks on either side of the teepee. Next, stack sticks on the other two sides so that the ends overlap in a log-cabin style. Continue until you are five layers high.

7. Add one or two sticks to the top of the cabin to form a "roof." Do not place too

many branches on top of the cabin or you
will suffocate the fire.

8. Light a match and place it inside the teepee
   so that it lights the kindling.

9. If built properly, the kindling will burn and
   the teepee will ignite the cabin.

10. If the fire needs help spreading, you should
    encourage it by adding kindling and sticks.
    You can also fan the fire at the base to help
    it spread.

11. Fuel the fire with increasingly larger sticks
    and logs. Remember that larger logs will
    require sufficient time to heat before
    burning.

12. When you are finished with the fire, let
    the fire and logs burn down. Then, pour
    several buckets of water on the fire (even if
    it looks like it has extinguished). If it still
    smokes, shovel some dirt onto the ashes.

Poker Hierarchy and Glossary

Which ranks higher, a straight or a flush? Before you take your run at the World Series of Poker, it's good to know the answer. Here's the ranking of poker hands in a standard game, from best to worst.

- **Royal Flush:** Ace, king, queen, jack, and ten of the same suit
- **Straight Flush:** Any five cards of the same suit in numerical order
- **Four of a Kind:** Four cards with the same number
- **Full House:** Three cards of the same number and two cards of the same number
- **Flush:** Any five cards of the same suit
- **Straight:** Any five cards in numerical order
- **Three of a Kind:** Three cards with the same number
- **Two Pair:** Two cards with the same number and another two cards with the same number

- **Two of a Kind:** Two cards with the same number

- In all cases, the higher numerical value takes precedence if there is a tie. For example, two aces beat two nines.

Here are some key poker terms that you may hear throughout the course of a game. Obviously, you'll want to understand these terms *before* you start wagering your hard-earned money.

- **Pot:** The pile of money in the center of the table. It's what you're trying to win.

- **Ante:** A small contribution from each player (before the cards are dealt) to establish the pot. The ante is typically not used in a Texas Hold 'Em–style game.

- **Big blind:** The larger of two forced bets in a Texas Hold 'Em–style game made before the cards are dealt. This is equivalent to a full first-round bet.

- **Flop:** The first three community cards placed face up at the same time in a game of Hold 'Em.

- **No limit:** A version of poker in which a player can bet as much as he'd like when it is his turn to wager.

- **River:** The fifth and final community card placed face up in a game of Hold 'Em.

- **Small blind:** The smaller of the two forced bets in a Hold 'Em–style game made before the cards are dealt. This is typically equivalent to one-third of the full first-round bet.

- **Turn:** The fourth community card placed face up in a game of Hold 'Em.

Toolbox Essentials

You may never be called upon to build a house—but when the cute girl next door loses her earring in the drain trap, shouldn't you be ready to lend a hand? Here's the bare minimum of what every guy should have in his toolbox.

- A tape measure
- Carpenter's level
- Claw hammer
- A stud finder
- Flat-head and Philips-head screwdrivers
- Nails and screws of varying sizes
- A monkey wrench or wrench set
- Allen wrenches
- A set of pliers (including slip-joint pliers with toothed jaws)
- A handsaw
- Utility knife with retractable blade
- A pair of work gloves
- Spray can of WD-40

- Duct tape and/or electrical tape
- Safety goggles
- Variable-speed reversible drill
- A staple gun with 1/2-inch staples
- Sandpaper
- Superglue, wood glue, and tacky glue
- A flashlight

Tips:

- Every tool you buy is a long-term investment. A good hammer should last a lifetime. Buy from a retailer you can trust, and invest in quality products.

- Add a small notebook to your toolbox and use it to record important data about your home. Keep a record of various paint colors so you can match them in the future. Note the last time you changed the batteries in your smoke detectors. List the specs of any unusual light bulbs used throughout your home. While you're at it, you may as well include the date of your wedding anniversary— every reminder helps.

How to Hang a Picture Frame

The art of hanging the picture should be as skilled as the art inside the frame.

1. Select the location. Don't hang one small picture on a large wall. Try to hang the frame so that it extends or matches the lines of furniture or windows (i.e., a long frame above a long sofa). Make certain that there is plenty of room for the frame.

2. Hold the frame up to the spot where it will be hung and mark the top with a pencil. The frame should be placed so that the middle is at eye level.

3. Select an appropriate hook. A nail-and-hook is fine for smaller frames. But if you're hanging a larger frame, be sure you are nailing directly into a wall stud (use a stud finder to locate one). Or buy some hollow-wall anchors, which grip the drywall more securely and distribute the picture's weight.

4. Measure the space from the top of the frame to the hanging mechanism. If it is

a wire, make sure you pull the wire taut before measuring.

5. Measure down that same distance from your original pencil mark on the wall. Make a new marking.

6. Nail or drill your hook into that new marking.

7. Hang and straighten the frame.

How to Jump-Start a Car

A dead battery is an easy thing to fix—provided that you've got a set of jumper cables in the trunk. (You *do* have jumper cables in your trunk, right?)

1. Refer to your car's owner's manual. It may provide important information on the particulars of your specific car. Some newer models require you to use special lugs designed for jump-starting, instead of connecting directly to the battery.

2. Recruit a driver with a working automobile. Park the working automobile beside your car so that the two batteries are as close as possible. Be sure the two cars are not touching each other.

3. Put both cars in park with the emergency brake engaged. Turn the cars off and remove the keys.

4. Pop the hoods of both cars.

5. Attach the red-handled (positive) jumper cable clamp to the positive terminal on the fully charged battery.

6. Attach the red-handled (positive) clamp at the other end of the jumper cable to the positive terminal on the dead battery.

7. Ground the black-handled (negative) jumper cable clamp to an exposed piece of clean metal on the dead car's engine—usually a nice shiny bolt will do the trick.

8. Attach the black-handled (negative) clamp at the other end of the jumper cable to the negative terminal on the charged battery.

9. Start the working automobile, and allow it to run for 2 to 3 minutes.

10. Start the car with the dead battery. If the engine starts, wait 3 or 4 minutes, and then remove the clamps one at a time in reverse order. Allow the "jumped" car to run for at least 30 minutes before turning it off, to ensure that the battery is fully charged.

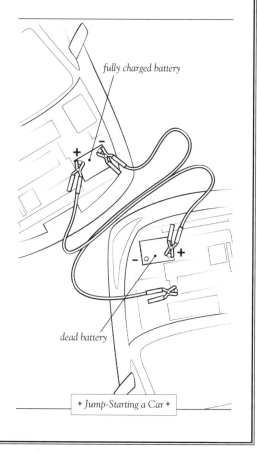

fully charged battery

dead battery

✦ *Jump-Starting a Car* ✦

How to Change a Flat Tire

Sure, you can call roadside assistance. But in the hour you wait for the tow truck to arrive, you can probably change the tire yourself and be back on the road.

1. Drive to a safe, flat, dry area. Driving on a flat tire may damage your car, so do not prolong the trip longer than necessary. But be certain you are all the way off the road.

2. Locate your spare tire and jack. In many vehicles, these will be hidden underneath the upholstery in the trunk. Note that many modern vehicles now include a "donut" instead of a full-size spare; this miniature tire is designed to get you only to the nearest service station. It should not be used for extended traveling.

3. Set the car in park and engage the emergency break. Place a large rock or piece of wood in front of and behind the tire opposite the flat to prevent the car from rolling.

3. Remove the hubcap and loosen the lug nuts with a four-way wrench. Loosen—but do not remove—the lug nut nearest the top of the tire.

5. Place the jack under the car. Consult the owner's manual for the proper placement of the jack. Never place the jack under any material that looks like it might bend, crumple, or collapse.

6. Use the jack to raise the car.

7. Remove the last lug and the tire.

8. Place the new tire on the mating surface. Replace the lugs and tighten them by hand.

9. Spin the tire a few times to make sure it turns properly.

10. Use the jack to lower the car, and then remove the jack.

11. Tighten the lugs using the four-way wrench.

The Only Knot You'll Ever Need to Know

How dependable is the bowline knot? Consider that the Federal Aviation Administration recommends its use when tying down light aircraft. And if it's good enough for securing a Cessna, you better believe it'll keep your canoe from drifting away. The bowline knot is so simple, even children can tie it. In fact, they often learn by using this basic mnemonic:

1. **This is the rabbit hole.** Make a loop in your rope.

2. **Out comes the rabbit.** Pull one end of the rope through the loop.

3. **It runs around the tree.** Wrap the end you pulled through the loop around the other end.

4. **And hops back into the hole.** Pull it back through the loop, and tighten the knot.

This is the rabbit hole.

Out comes the rabbit.

It runs around the tree.

And hops back into the hole.

✦ *The Bowline Knot* ✦

How to Cast a Fishing Rod

Whether you're deep-sea fishing on a special bachelor party weekend or spending a day on a stream with old Pop-Pop, casting a fishing rod is the definitive skill every man should know.

1. Check to ensure you have enough clearance to properly cast the line.

2. Firmly grip the rod near the base with your casting (dominant) hand. The joint attaching the reel to the rod should be between your middle and ring fingers.

3. If you are using an open-faced rod, flip the bail with your other hand while holding the line against the rod with the index finger on your casting hand.

4. With your cast arm in line with the rod, point the rod at your target. Keep the tip raised slightly to eye level.

5. Bending at the elbow, raise your casting hand until the rod is parallel to your body (Figure A).

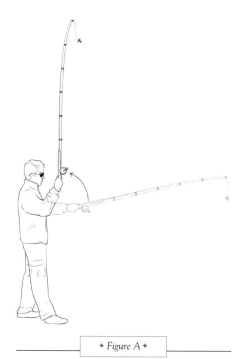

✦ Figure A ✦

Raise your casting hand until the rod is parallel to your body.

6. Again, bending at the elbow, bring the rod forward with a slight snap in the wrist (Figure B). When you get about 15 degrees from your starting position, release your index finger's grasp on the line. This will propel the line out into the water.

Tips:

- Your strength does not affect the length of your cast. It's all in the technique. Many men practice their casting in fields or parks to make the most of their time on the water.

- If you find that you enjoy casting more than fishing, consider enrolling in the International Casting Sport Federation (ICSF), which was founded in 1955 and has member associations in countries around the world.

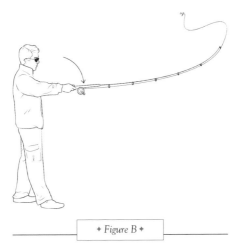

✦ Figure B ✦

*Bring the rod forward with a slight snap
in the wrist.*

Twelve Famous Playboy Playmates

Name	First Centerfold Appearance
Pamela Anderson	February 1990
Carmella DeCesare	April 2003
Jayne Mansfield	February 1955
Jenny McCarthy	October 1993

Famous (or Infamous) for

Roles on *Baywatch* and *Home Improvement*; her bootlegged sex tape with husband and Mötley Crüe drummer Tommy Lee; a memorable cameo in *Borat*.

Placing second in the World Wrestling Entertainment RAW Diva Search; marrying Tampa Bay quarterback Jeff Garcia.

Her tragic 1967 car accident, in which her vehicle crashed into the rear of a tractor trailer; the "Mansfield Guard," now standard equipment on all tractor trailers, was named in her honor.

Numerous TV and film appearances including *Jenny*, a short-lived NBC sitcom; her work as a spokesperson for families affected by autism.

Name	First Centerfold Appearance
Shanna Moakler	December 2001
Kelly Monaco	April 1997
Marilyn Monroe	December 1953
Bettie Page	January 1955

Famous (or Infamous) for

Her on-and-off marriage to drummer Travis Barker, which was chronicled on the MTV reality show *Meet the Barkers*; reuniting with Barker after a plane crash nearly killed him in 2008.

Winning two daytime Emmy Awards for her performances on *General Hospital* and *Port Charles*; winning the first season of *Dancing with the Stars*.

Performances in *Some Like It Hot*, *Gentlemen Prefer Blondes*, and other films; marriages with Joe DiMaggio and Arthur Miller; being the first playmate in the first issue of *Playboy*.

Pin-up icon famous for photographs depicting bondage or sadomasochistic themes; her conversion to Christianity (and work as a missionary) in the 1960s.

Name	First Centerfold Appearance
Anna Nicole Smith	May 1992
Dorothy Stratten	August 1979
Shannon Tweed	November 1981
Victoria Zdrok	October 1994

Famous (or Infamous) for

Modeling for Guess jeans; marrying octogenarian billionaire J. Howard Marshall; an inheritance case that went all the way to the U.S. Supreme Court.

Her tragic murder in 1980 by her estranged husband, Paul Snider; her life story was adapted into the 1983 film *Star-80* by acclaimed theater director Bob Fosse.

Appearances in numerous "erotic thrillers" with titles like *Victim of Desire*, *Stormy Nights*, and *Body Chemistry 4: Full Exposure*; her long-term relationship with Kiss frontman Gene Simmons.

Being the second model to appear in both *Playboy* and *Penthouse* as a centerfold (Pet of the Month in June 2002 and Pet of the Year in 2004); being a sex therapist, psychologist, and attorney.

How to Hold a Baby

As a general rule, women admire men who are comfortable with babies. So hold your head high and try the simple "cradle hold" (Figure A).

1. Place the baby's head in the crook of your arm (the inside bend of the elbow).

2. Secure the baby's body with that hand.

3. Use your free arm to support the baby's bottom.

4. To calm a fussy baby, rock your arms gently back and forth.

And if you really want to show off, hold the baby in the "potato sack" carry (Figure B).

1. Position yourself behind a baby in the face-down position.

2. Slide your dominant hand between the baby's legs, resting it palm up on the baby's chest.

3. Use your other hand to secure the baby.

4. Scoop up the baby and carry at your side, as if holding a football.

+ Figure A +

+ Figure B +

For older babies who have greater head and neck control, the hip hold is also recommended (Figure C).

1. Rest the baby's bottom on your hip, with his chest resting against your side.

2. Wrap that same arm around the baby's bottom and lower back.

Another option for older babies is to hold them so that they can see what is going on—the "face-out hold" (Figure D).

1. Support the baby's back by placing it against your chest so that the baby is facing forward.

2. Place one arm under the baby's bottom.

3. Place the other arm across the baby's chest.

Figure C

Figure D

Tips for Selecting a Good Cigar

We know you know this, but it bears repeating: These things'll kill ya. So don't shorten your lifespan by smoking crappy cigars. Get yourself a good one.

- **Consider the strength of the tobacco.** Most connoisseurs agree that the best tobacco plants are grown in the Caribbean.

- **Consider the filler.** Choose a cigar with long, bundled leaves so that the filler doesn't break apart in your mouth.

- **Consider the wrapper.** It should be oily and smooth. Avoid a cigar with extreme color variations or cracks in the wrapper.

- **Consider the texture.** Gently pinch the cigar in several spots along its length. Avoid a cigar with lumps or soft spots.

- **Consider the length and thickness.** This is strictly a personal preference, but obviously larger cigars will require more time to smoke.

Fifteen Wardrobe Essentials

With these items in your closet, you'll be prepared for virtually any situation.

1. **Shoes.** Of all your measurements, your shoe size will remain the most constant over the course of your life. Find a quality pair of black leather loafers and make the investment.

2. **A suit.** If you purchase just one, choose a classic dark suit that will lend itself to a variety of events. Spend a few extra bucks to have the suit properly tailored.

3. **A tuxedo.** Celebrate your twenty-fifth birthday by purchasing a classic two-button tuxedo with notch lapels. This look never goes out of style. In the long run, it's smarter to own than to rent.

4. **Dress shirts.** A white shirt is a safe and classic option. Supplement with other colors and patterns that complement your personal style. Dry clean your dress shirts without

starch and have them pressed by hand. They will look crisper and last longer.

5. **Belts.** Your belt color should match your shoes. Black with black. Brown with brown.

6. **Socks.** These are a subtle, understated means for expressing your personality. Women notice them and admire the attention to detail. Choose from solids, stripes, argyle, or polka dots, to name just a few of the available patterns.

7. **Ties.** Like socks, your tie can say a lot about your personality. Purchase at least one new tie every year to keep up with trends.

8. **Blue jeans.** Darker jeans look more formal and can be adapted to a variety of situations. No rips. No fraying.

9. **Khaki pants.** A darker color allows you to transition from the office to a night on the town without changing clothes.

10. **T-shirts.** A white T-shirt paired with jeans or khakis makes for a nice, classic, casual look. Supplement your wardrobe with

three or four V-necks and rounded-collar T-shirts of various colors.

11. **Collared shirts.** A polo shirt is a classic and versatile look. It can be layered under a sports jacket or worn with jeans.

12. **Sweaters.** Sweaters are good for layering over a collared shirt in the winter or as a stand-alone item in the spring. A charcoal grey V-neck goes well with a suit, jeans, or pants.

13. **Underwear.** Choose from boxers, briefs, or bikini briefs, based on your own comfort. Keep a few in mint condition for special occasions.

14. **Sneakers.** You need two pairs: one for the gym, and one for a stylish night out.

15. **A briefcase.** Choose a briefcase that matches your work attire. A backpack is fine for jeans, but a leather bag is a must when wearing a suit.

The Perfect Attire for Every Occasion

Is there a difference between black-tie optional and semiformal? Surprisingly, yes.

- **White tie:** black tailcoat with silk facings and a white shirt, collar, waistcoat, and bow tie
- **Black tie:** tuxedo
- **Black-tie optional:** tuxedo or formal suit
- **Semiformal:** formal suit or sports jacket with a tie and trousers
- **Business:** formal suit or sports jacket with a tie and trousers
- **Business casual:** trousers and a dress shirt
- **Casual:** jeans and the type of shirt depend on the attendees

How to Tie a Tie

In today's business-casual world, ties are increasingly less common—but there will always be weddings, funerals, and graduation ceremonies. With a basic four-in-hand knot, you'll always be prepared.

1. Lift your collar.

2. Wrap the tie around your neck under the collar, with the wide end on the right side. The wide end should lie twice as long as the narrow end.

3. Cross the wide end over the narrow end and back underneath twice (Figures A, B, and C).

✦ *Figure A* ✦

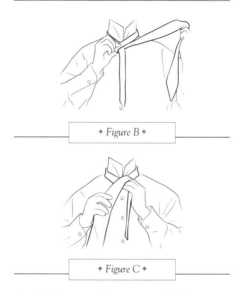

✦ Figure B ✦

✦ Figure C ✦

4. On the second pass, instead of wrapping back around, push the wide end through the loop made near your neck (Figure D).

5. Pass the wide end through the knot near your neck (Figure E).

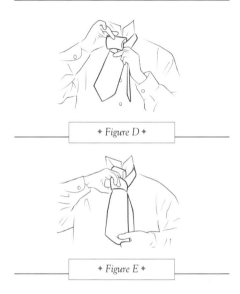

+ Figure D +

+ Figure E +

6. Keep the wide end on top of the narrow end as you pull it through.

7. Tighten by drawing the knot toward your neck while holding the narrow end with your other hand.

◆ *Figure F* ◆

8. Straighten. The tie should hang to your belt buckle with the top lying longer than the bottom (Figure F). If that doesn't happen, untie, adjust the ends accordingly, and try again.

How to Sew On a Button

Why should a guy know how to sew on a button? Because it's cheaper than buying a new shirt.

1. Select a button and thread that match the article of clothing. Thread that is slightly darker than the fabric is ideal, because the stitches will blend better (lighter thread stands out more).

2. Thread a needle so that there is 1 foot (30 cm) of thread on both sides of the needle. If you have trouble, lick the end of the thread before inserting it through the needle's eye.

3. Knot the two ends of the thread together.

4. Position the button on the fabric, making sure that it is aligned with the corresponding buttonhole as well as the other buttons on the garment.

5. Starting from the underside of the fabric, push the needle through the fabric and one

hole of the button. Pull the thread all the way through.

6. Push the needle down through the next hole in the button and through the fabric, pulling the thread all the way through.

7. Bring the needle back through the fabric and a hole in the button, and repeat this process about ten times to ensure that the button will stay put (Figure A).

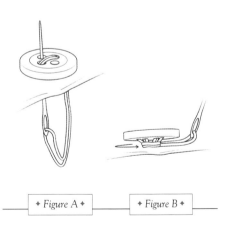

+ *Figure A* +   + *Figure B* +

8. Then pull the needle and thread through the fabric under the button, but not through a hole. Pull the thread all the way through. Wrap it around the thread that holds the button to the fabric three or four times (Figure B).

9. Push the needle back through to the underside of the fabric and pull it taught. Angling the needle almost flat against the fabric, push it through the fabric but not to the surface (Figure C).

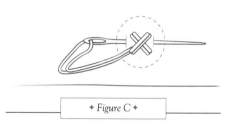

✦ Figure C ✦

10. Before you pull the thread taught, pull the needle through the loop in the thread a few times to create a knot. Repeat

several times, overlaying stitches to secure the knot (Figure D).

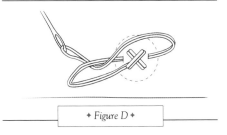

+ *Figure D* +

11. Trim off excess thread.

Tip: Place a penny under the edge of the button while you sew to ensure there is enough slack for the button to be pulled through its corresponding buttonhole and accommodate the additional layer of fabric.

How to Shave Properly

In a world full of high-tech electric shavers with free-floating pulsonic blades and whisper-silent pop-up trimmers, does anyone really need to know how to shave with a plain old razor blade? The answer will seem obvious when you arrive in Houston for the big account meeting—but your luggage is rerouted to Cleveland. All you need to save the day is a can of shaving cream and one very sharp piece of metal.

1. Wash your face with soap and water. To soften your skin, wet a washcloth with warm water and hold it to your face for 30 seconds. This will ensure a much smoother shave.

2. Using a shaving brush or your hand, apply the shaving cream over the area you wish to shave. If you don't have shaving cream, hair conditioner makes a good emergency substitute.

3. Be sure to use a new (or relatively new) razor blade. Dragging a dull piece of

metal across your face is a surefire way to sabotage your appearance.

4. Starting on one side of your face, shave from the top of the beard line down to your jawline in one even stroke. Move with the grain of the hair. Be sure to hold the razor at a 45-degree angle or less to reduce nicks and cuts. Rinse the razor between strokes and continue with the rest of your face in the same manner.

5. Starting on one side of your neck, shave from the hairline on your neck up to your jawline in one even stroke. Continue with the rest of your chin/neck in the same manner. You may want to pull your skin taut with your free hand to ensure a closer shave.

6. Rinse the shaving cream from your face and look for spots you have missed. Pay careful attention to the areas around your mouth, nostrils, and sideburns.

7. Soothe nicks and cuts by splashing your face with cold water; it will often cease the

flow of blood. If you are prone to shaving injuries, invest in a styptic pencil, which constricts the blood vessels around an open cut.

7. Upon completion, pat your face with a clean towel and apply a moisturizer to prevent your skin from drying out.

Tip: A straight razor offers the closest shave possible, but using one is extremely dangerous. Shaving with a straight razor requires tremendous patience and practice—which may be in short supply at six-thirty in the morning, when you're racing to catch your train. If you'd like to experience this classic shave, ask a trained professional—your barber—to do it.

How to Perform a Proper Push-Up

Before you drop and give me twenty, learn how to do push-ups properly—and most effectively.

1. Lie chest-down on the floor. Place your palms flat on the floor, shoulder-width apart. (Increasing this distance will make the push-ups easier; decreasing it will make them harder.) Your chin and the balls of your feet should be touching the floor. Breathe in.

2. Straighten your arms as you exhale and push your body away from the floor. Your palms should stay in the same position. Your legs should stay pressed together. Your body should form a straight line from head to heel.

3. Pause when your arms are at full extension.

4. Bend your arms as you inhale and lower yourself to the ground. Touch your chest and knees to the floor. Repeat.

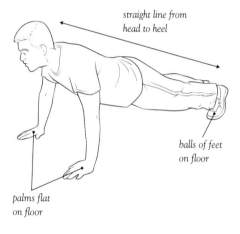

straight line from head to heel

balls of feet on floor

palms flat on floor

✦ A Proper Push-Up ✦

Note: You should aim to perform at least 20 push-ups in one minute.

How to Perform Abdominal Crunches

Forget about old-fashioned sit-ups; most experts now recognize that they're hard on your back and an inefficient form of exercise. If you really want to hone a six-pack, try doing some abdominal crunches instead.

1. Lie on your back with your feet flat on the floor. You will work more efficiently (and comfortably) on a mat or carpet. Bend your knees so they form an inverted V. Have a partner secure your feet to the floor. The distance between your feet should be as wide as your hips. Place your hands behind your head; your elbows should be pointing out.

2. Curl up so that your head, neck, and shoulder blades leave the floor. Do not allow your arms to push you up; instead, leave the heavy lifting to your abdominal muscles. If you're doing it right, you'll feel it.

3. Pause and then lower yourself to a starting position. Repeat.

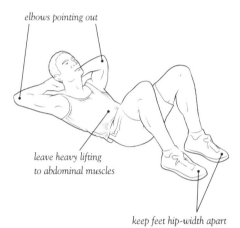

elbows pointing out

leave heavy lifting to abdominal muscles

keep feet hip-width apart

✦ Proper Crunches ✦

Note: You should aim to perform at least 40 abdominal crunches in one minute.

How to Perform a Proper Pull-Up

Combine this exercise with push-ups and abdominal crunches, and you'll have one hell of an upper body.

1. Stand under a pull-up bar. If you don't have gym equipment handy, you can use the limb of a tree.

2. Grab the bar using a pronated (overhand) grip. If you require assistance reaching the bar, use a stepstool or chair that you can later kick away.

3. Let your body hang for a moment. Relax your shoulders and try not to arch your back.

4. Pull your chest toward the bar by bending your arms in a single smooth movement. Keep your torso straight without jerking your muscles or flailing your legs.

5. Raise your body until your chin reaches the bar. Pause for a moment, then lower yourself back down. Repeat.

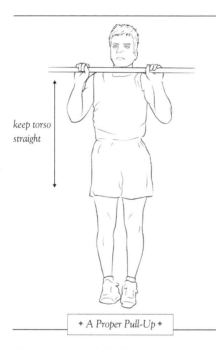

keep torso straight

✦ A Proper Pull-Up ✦

Note: Some men lack the upper-body strength to complete even a single pull-up. If you can complete 15 of these in a minute, we salute you.

How to Throw a Punch

It's stupid to go looking for a fight. But when a fight comes looking for you, it's smart to be prepared.

1. Stand with your feet shoulder-width apart and your knees slightly bent.

2. Make a fist with both hands and bring the fists down to waist level. Your fingers should be facing up, with your thumb across them. Your elbows should point straight behind you.

3. Aim for the abdomen or rib cage.

4. Bring your dominant hand forward, rotating your fist past upright into a 45-degree position. Lead with your knuckles and extend your arm fully outward.

5. Drive your non-dominant elbow backward for extra power.

6. Retract your arm before your elbow is fully extended and locked.

Drive opposite elbow backward for extra power

Aim for the abdomen or rib cage

✦ A Proper Punch ✦

How to Fart in Public and Get Away With It

We've all been there. The urge creeps up. The panic sets in. What do I do? Where do I go? If you can't escape to a private location, here are a few tips to consider:

- Move to the noisiest place you can find. Noise will mask the sound.

- Move to the most crowded place you can find. For starters, a crowd usually results in a certain level of noise. More importantly, a large number of people will help deflect blame.

- At the moment of release, create a noisy distraction such as coughing, slamming a drawer, or dropping a heavy object.

- Work with an accomplice. You can do this by agreeing upon a code word with a close friend. Your accomplice will be required to create a diversion whenever you speak the code word. You should agree to return the favor for him.

- At the first natural opportunity, exit the area. Walk confidently but not too quickly. You don't want to look like you're fleeing a crime scene.

- If you cannot leave the area, consider passing the blame. Small children, pets, and the elderly are obvious targets. Whatever you do, never blame it on a woman.

Tip: You can avoid this situation completely by making smart dietary choices. Of course, no two digestive systems are alike, so experiment with different foods to determine which ones affect you the most. As a general rule, it's wise to avoid the following "high-risk" foods before any party or social function: beans (particularly baked beans), broccoli, brussel sprouts, cabbage, cauliflower, chili, grains, and fiber (especially pumpernickel bread), onions, oysters, and salads.

The Perfect Tip for Every Occasion

Who	How Much
Airport valet	$1 per bag
Barber/Hairdresser	10–15 percent
Bartender	$1 per drink
Coat check/valet	$1–$2 per coat
Doorman	$1 per bag
Food delivery	10 percent
Furniture delivery and movers	$5–$10 per person

Notes

Consider adding an extra dollar or two if the bags are particularly heavy or cumbersome, or if the weather is inclement.

If you see the same barber regularly, consider giving him a holiday tip equal to the cost of one haircut.

There's no good reason to stiff your bartender.

Most coat-check personnel are paid less than minimum wage and depend upon tips.

For hailing cabs, helping with packages, etc.

$2 minimum

You may choose to increase this amount if the delivery requires special handling or assembly.

Who	How Much
Golf caddie	$3 per bag
Hotel bellhop	$1 per bag
Hotel maid	$2–$5 per night
Server	15 percent
Shoe shine	$2
Taxi driver	10–20 percent of the fare

Notes

10–20 percent if he actually caddies
your round.

Add a dollar or two if he shows you the room.

Depends on the quality of the hotel.

20 percent if your party is six or more or if
you feel the server did an exceptional job. In
Europe, gratuity is often included in your bill.

Add a few dollars if he gives you a hot
stock tip.

If you pay by credit card, remember that the
cabbie is charged the card-handling fee.

How to Open a Beer Bottle Without an Opener

Sooner or later, you're bound to find yourself with a perfectly good six-pack—and no way to open the bottles. Fear not: Everything you need is right at hand.

1. Grab another beer bottle.

2. Place the bottle you wish to open in your non-dominant hand. Hold that bottle at its neck in the upright position. Hold the second bottle horizontally by the label.

3. Fit the shallow ridge found at midcap of the opener bottle under the bottom edge of the other bottle's cap. Using the opener bottle for leverage, press up and pry off the other cap.

4. The goal is to pry the cap away from the bottle. There are a variety of other items that can accomplish this task, including a screwdriver, envelope opener, knife, belt buckle, lighter, and table top.

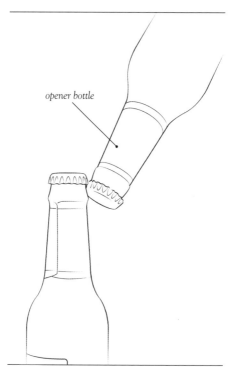

opener bottle

Using the opener bottle as a level, press up
and pry off the other cap.

How to Shotgun a Beer

If you're going to attend a bachelor party—or any accredited four-year college or university in North America—you may be challenged to shotgun a beer. We recommend that you do this outside (or at least over a sink), since it can be very messy.

1. Hold a beer can at a 45-degree angle so that the top is nearly facing the ground (Figure A).

2. Use a sharp object, such as a pen or a knife, to puncture a hole in the side of the can near the bottom (Figure B).

3. Place your mouth over the hole and turn the can upright. Suck the beer through the hole until little or no additional beer will come out (Figure C).

4. With your mouth still on the hole, open the can from the top, as you normally would. Drink as quickly as you can (Figure D). A 12-ounce can of beer will empty itself in approximately 15 seconds.

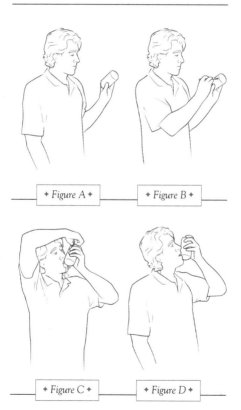

✦ Figure A ✦   *✦ Figure B ✦*

✦ Figure C ✦   *✦ Figure D ✦*

Elements of a Basic Bar

You never know when a party is going to break out. Be prepared for any type of occasion with the elements of a basic bar.

Utensils

- A jigger measure
- A glass or plastic stirring rod
- A cocktail shaker with a good lid
- An ice bucket with tongs
- A corkscrew
- A bottle/can opener

Glassware (recommended 4–6 of each)

- Cocktail or martini glasses
- White-wine glasses
- Red-wine glasses
- Champagne glasses
- Snifters
- Pint or pilsner glasses
- Highball glasses

- Rocks glasses
- Shot glasses

Wine and Spirits

- 1 liter of vodka
- 1 liter of dry vermouth
- 1 liter of gin
- 1 liter of Bourbon
- 1 liter of whiskey
- 1 liter of rum
- 1 liter of Scotch whiskey
- 1 liter of triple sec
- 1 liter of tequila
- 1 bottle of white wine
- 1 bottle of red wine
- 12 bottles of beer

Mixers

- 1 bottle of grenadine
- 1 bottle of cola
- 1 bottle of club soda

- 1 bottle of tonic water
- Assorted juices (orange, grapefruit, cranberry, lime, and tomato)
- Hot sauce
- Plenty of ice

Garnishes

- Green olives
- Cocktail onions
- Maraschino cherries
- Lemon
- Lime
- Apple
- Orange or grapefruit
- Carrot and celery sticks
- Sugar, salt, and pepper

Drinks That Change Your Breath . . .

. . . For the Better:

- Gin and tonic
- Gimlet
- Vodka and cranberry
- Any drink with citrus

. . . For the Worse:

- Beer
- Any sweet drink
- Any drink with milk
- Any drink with chocolate

Tip: If you have any doubt about the freshness of your breath, ask the bartender to prepare dos mojitos for you and your companion. These popular rum-based cocktails are served with an abundance of fresh mint. Chewing the leaves (and even the stems) will eliminate any trace of halitosis.

Two Cocktails for Women

If there's one cocktail most women can agree upon, it's this one.

- **Cosmopolitan:**

    Combine ³/₄ oz vodka, ¹/₂ oz triple sec, 1 oz cranberry juice, and ¹/₂ oz lime juice with ice in a cocktail mixer. Shake and strain into an iced martini glass.

Of course, there's always the chance you'll find one of the few women in the world who does not like Cosmopolitans. Not a problem. Make an apple martini instead.

- **Apple Martini:**

    Combine 2 oz vodka, 1¹/₂ oz apple schnapps, and ¹/₂ oz lemon juice with ice in a cocktail mixer. Shake and strain into a martini glass. Garnish with an apple slice.

Two Cocktails for Your Parents

Show your parents that you have matured past college by mixing up a gin martini.

- **Gin Martini:**

  Combine 1²/₃ oz gin and ²/₃ oz dry vermouth with ice in a cocktail mixer. Shake and strain into an iced martini glass. Serve with an olive.

And if your father doesn't like gin, don't worry. Make the old man a vodka gimlet instead.

- **Vodka Gimlet:**

  Combine 1½ oz vodka, 1 oz lime juice, and 1 teaspoon powdered sugar with ice in a cocktail mixer. Shake and strain into a martini glass.

Two Cocktails for a Party

This may be the greatest party drink of all time: beer and margarita in a single glass. Here's how to whip up a party-sized pitcher.

- **Beer Margarita:**

    Pour the following ingredients into a blender: 1½ cups tequila, ½ cup Grand Marnier, ⅓ bottle beer, 1 can frozen lemonade concentrate, the juice of one lime, the juice of half a lemon, and ½ cup agave nectar. Fill the blender with ice and blend until smooth. Pour into margarita or rocks glasses.

A more traditional alternative is the hurricane, a rum-based drink popularized by New Orleans tavern owner Pat O'Brien during the 1940s.

- **Hurricane:**

    Combine 1 oz vodka, 1 oz amaretto, 1 oz triple sec, 1 oz light rum, 1 oz gin, and ¼ oz grenadine in a large cup ¾ full with ice. Fill with equal parts pineapple and grapefruit juice. Serve in highball glasses.

How to Win a Drink at a Bar

Is there anything better than taking advantage of your drunken friends and earning a free beer in the process?

1. Bet your buddy that you can finish three pints of beer before he can finish three shots. There are only two stipulations: He needs to give you a one-pint head start, and neither of you can touch the other guy's glasses.

2. Drink your first beer.

3. When finished, place the cup upside down over one of his shot glasses.

4. Drink the other two pints at your leisure. Since he can't touch your glass to remove it, you now have all the time in the world.

How to Order a Bottle of Wine

Ordering a bottle of wine can be intimidating, especially if you don't know the proper etiquette. Here are a few tips on selecting a wine and instructions for participating in the tasting ritual.

1. Consider what you will be eating with the wine. Reds typically complement heavier meals, such as meat and pasta. Whites pair better with lighter meals, such as chicken, fish, and salads. If you want to really show off, try pairing your cuisine with a wine from the same region of the world.

2. Select a wine from the menu that meets your price range. A more expensive bottle doesn't necessarily translate into a better-tasting bottle.

3. When in doubt, ask the server or sommelier for advice. Be sure to mention the type of wine you are looking for and your approximate budget. There's no need to mention dollar amounts. Simply point to a wine on the menu and say, "This is

what I would ordinarily order, but I'm interested in something different this evening. What can you recommend?"

Once you have made your selection, the server will bring the wine to your table and begin the tasting ritual.

1. The server will present the bottle with the label facing out. Confirm that it is the bottle you ordered.

2. After opening the bottle, the server will present you with the cork. Inspect the cork to ensure that it is not damaged, cracked, or dried out. Do not smell it.

3. The server will then pour a small amount of wine into your glass. Swirl it to release the aroma: Grasp the stem of the glass and, keeping the base firmly on the table, move the glass in small circles.

4. Bring the glass to your nose to smell the bouquet. Confirm that it doesn't smell rancid or musty.

5. Taste the wine. Confirm its flavor and indicate that the server may pour the rest of the glasses. If anything about the bottle is unsatisfactory, express your concerns immediately. A good server will handle the situation without making you uncomfortable. Choose another bottle or ask the server to recommend a personal favorite.

Facts and Notes About Wine

Most common red grape types and their characteristics:

- **Cabernet Sauvignon:** Full-bodied wines with a toasty cedar taste.
- **Merlot:** Smooth wines with the flavor of plums.
- **Pinot Noir:** Earthy-tasting wines that evoke the flavor of cherries.
- **Syrah:** Intense, almost meaty flavored wines with a taste of black pepper.
- **Zinfandel:** Fruity, berry-flavored wines often mixed with green grapes to make rose wines.

Most common white grape types and their characteristics:

- **Chardonnay:** Popular wines with an aroma and taste of tropical fruit.
- **Pinot Grigio:** Crisp, refreshing, dry wines.
- **Riesling:** Sweeter wines with a floral aroma and an undertone of peaches.

- **Sauvignon Blanc:** Citrus-y and acidic wines with a grassy flavor.

Ideal temperature for serving wine:

- **Red:** 65°F (18°C)
- **White:** 55°F (13°C)
- **Champagne:** 45°F (7°C)

On the rare occasion that you do not finish a bottle of red or white wine, it can be saved. Move the wine to a capped container that will be completely filled with the wine—this removes oxygen, the main spoiling agent. Refrigerate.

The World's Only Funny Knock-Knock Joke

Knock, Knock.
Who's there?

An interrupting cow.
An interrupt—

MOO!!!

An Obligatory Joke About Changing a Light Bulb

Question: How many Harvard graduates does it take to change a light bulb?

Answer: Just one. He holds the light bulb, and the world revolves around him.

A Good Joke for a Kid

Question: What do you call a dinosaur with one eye?

Answer: A do-you-think-he-saw-us.

Another Good Joke for a Kid

A duck walks into a store and asks for some lipstick.

The cashier says to the duck, "That'll be $1.49."

The duck says, "Put it on my bill!"

A Good Joke for a Date

Joe takes Kelly to a carnival on a blind date. Joe asks, "What would you like to do first?" and Kelly replies, "I want to get weighed." So they visit the weight-guesser, who predicts that Kelly weighs 130 pounds. Since she weighs only 110 pounds, Kelly wins a stuffed animal.

So then Joe says, "What would you like to do next?" and again Kelly says, "I want to get weighed." He suggests the Ferris wheel and the rollercoaster but Kelly is adamant. So they return to the weight-guesser and this time, of course, the weight guesser has no trouble guessing Kelly's weight: 110 pounds.

"Maybe we should try the fun house," Joe suggests. "Or the swings."

Kelly insists, "I want to get weighed."

By this point, Joe is completely bewildered, so he fakes a headache and drives Kelly home. When she enters her apartment, her roommate Laura is waiting for her. "How was the date?" she asks.

"Oh, Wauwa, it was wousy!"

A Good Joke for the Guys

A guy enters a bar carrying an alligator.

He says to the other patrons, "Here's the deal. I'll open this alligator's mouth and insert my genitals. The gator will close his mouth for one minute, then open it, and I'll remove my unit unscathed. If it works, everyone buys me drinks."

The other patrons clap and cheer. It's a deal.

So the guy drops his pants and puts his privates in the gator's mouth. The gator closes its mouth. After a minute, the guy grabs a beer bottle and bangs the gator on the top of its head. The gator opens wide, and he removes his genitals unscathed. Everyone buys him drinks.

Then he says: "I'll pay $100 to anyone else who's willing to give it a try."

After a while, a hand goes up in the back of the bar. It's a woman.

"I'll try," she says. "But you have to promise not to hit me with the beer bottle."

A Good Joke for the Office

Three building contractors were touring the White House on the same day. One was from New York, another from Missouri, and the third from Florida.

At the end of the tour, the guard asked them what they did for a living. When they explained that they were contractors, the guard said, "Hey, we need to have our driveways re-paved. Why don't you guys take a look and give me your bids."

The Florida contractor took out his tape measure and pencil, did some measuring, and said, "I figure the job will run about $900: $400 for materials, $400 for my crew, and $100 profit for me."

Next, the Missouri contractor took out his tape measure and pencil, did some quick calculations, and said, "Looks like I can do this job for $700: $300 for materials, $300 for my crew, and $100 profit for me."

Finally, the guard asked the New York contractor for his bid. Without batting an eye, he said, "Twenty-seven hundred dollars."

The guard, incredulous, looked at him and said, "You didn't even measure like the other guys! How do you figure $2,700?"

"Easy," said the contractor from New York. "A thousand dollars for me, a thousand for you, and we hire the guy from Missouri."

How to Bet on Horses

You could walk up to the window and put your hard-earned cash on a horse named "Hard-Earned Cash." But if you want to win real money, follow these simple tips.

1. Pick the right horse(s). The race card will list information about all the horses in the race.

   a. The odds will give you a strong indication of how each horse will fare in that race. Note that 2–1 odds are better than 3–1 odds.

   b. The race card will indicate the last time the horse raced. To ensure that the horse is in racing shape, choose one that has raced within the past month.

   c. The number of horses in the race will give you a sense of the competition. Fewer horses means an easier path to victory.

   d. If the race card shows a C next to the horse's name, the horse has won on this track before. If the race card shows a D, the horse has won at this distance before.

2. Select the dollar amount you'd like to bet. Typically, the minimum you can bet on a horse is $2. The odds indicate the payout multiple for a win. A $2 bet on a horse with 2–1 odds pays $4 plus your original bet of $2. A $2 bet on a horse with 7–1 odds pays $14 plus your original bet of $2.

3. Select the type of bet. The most common types include

   a. **Straight bet to win:** Choose the horse that you think will finish first. ("I'd like ten dollars to win on number five.")

   b. **Straight bet to place:** Choose one horse that you think will finish first or second. ("I'd like ten dollars to place on number five.")

   c. **Straight bet to show:** Choose one horse that you think will finish first, second, or third. ("I'd like ten dollars to show on number five.")

d. Exacta bet: Choose the horses that you think will finish first and second in order. ("I'd like a ten dollar exacta on numbers three and five.")

e. Trifecta Bet: Choose the horses that you think will finish first, second, and third in order. ("I'd like a ten dollar trifecta on numbers three, five, and six.")

4. Bring all winning tickets to the cashier after the race. Losing tickets may be discarded.

How to Calculate Your Golf Handicap

Your golf handicap is the number of strokes you typically shoot over or under par on any given course. Thanks to the handicapping system, you can compete against (and perhaps even beat) first-rate players such as Tiger Woods. Good luck with that.

1. Gather the scorecards from your last five rounds. You will need three key pieces of information for each round: your scores, the course ratings, and the slope ratings.

2. For the first round, subtract the course rating from your score. Multiply the result by 113. Then divide this number by the slope rating to determine the differential.

3. Repeat this process for the other four rounds.

4. Multiply your lowest differential by 0.96 to get your handicap. This number will be subtracted from your score at the end of the game to calculate your final score.

Five Classic Golf Bets

If merely playing golf isn't challenging enough for your foursome, here are a couple of wagers designed to keep things interesting.

1. **Nassau:** Each golfer pays $2 to the winner on the front nine, the back nine, and the full eighteen. Select any scoring method you like.

2. **Acey-deucey:** The player with the lowest score (ace) on each hole is paid an agreed-upon amount by each of the other three players. The player with the highest score (deuce) on each hole pays the other three players an agreed-upon amount. If there's a tie (for ace or deuce), there is no payout. This will result in one big winner and one big loser for each hole.

3. **Round robin:** Pair up with a member of your foursome. Declare a winning tandem after six holes and switch your teams. Switch again after the twelfth hole.

4. **Arnies:** This common side bet is paid to any player who scores a par or better without landing his tee shot on the fairway. The round should be played with the intent to land on the fairway.

5. **Putt for dough:** The goal is to 1-putt. Once all balls are on the green, the ball farthest from the pin gets 4 points if the golfer 1-putts. The third farthest gets 3 points, the second farthest gets 2 points, and the closest gets 1 point. Points are only awarded for 1-putts. Anyone who 3-putts loses 1 point. Anyone who holes out from off the green receives 5 points. Tally the totals at the end of the game and pay out.

How to Ask for a Raise

The average guy thinks that he deserves more than he's earning. If you feel the same way, here's how to do something about it.

1. **Do your homework.** You should know what others in your field are earning, what you should be earning, and what your employer can afford to pay you. There are a variety of Internet resources and professional organizations available to help you understand the salary for your field. Factor in your experience and location with those resources to calculate what you should be earning. Finally, try to determine the financial health of your company, so you'll know if this is a good time to ask for a raise.

2. **Prepare your case.** Combine your research with a detailed report of what you have done for the company during your employment. Highlight key initiatives and the skills you possess that have made you a successful employee. Treat this as if you

were interviewing for a job and selling yourself to a prospective employer.

3. **Know the consequences.** What will you do if you don't receive the raise? What if your manager wants to negotiate a bit? Would you consider other benefits in exchange for a salary increase? Prepare for this discussion ahead of time, so you aren't blindsided at the meeting.

4. **Set up an appointment with your manager.** Be sure you are meeting in person. Aim for the end of the day in an office or a quiet conference room.

5. **Present your case.** Express your satisfaction with the company in general, and perhaps outline some of the goals you'd like to accomplish in the near future. Then name the salary that you feel is appropriate for your position and achievements. Consider proposing a number higher than you'd like, so you can negotiate as needed.

How to Negotiate

Whether your goal is a new mattress, a used car, or extra vacation days in a job contract, you need to remember that negotiation is a head game. To be the winner, you must control the situation—and that means being willing to walk away from the deal if you don't get what you want.

1. **Do your homework.** Get competitive pricing. Understand how the deal will work. And know what concessions you can make in your negotiation.

2. **Understand your goal and their goal.** You know what you want to accomplish. What's motivating the other party? Where do they want to end up? If possible, talk to other people in the industry beforehand, so you can gain additional perspective.

3. **Open with an extreme proposal.** Your initial proposal should be far enough away from your goal to allow for you to compromise and still come out a winner.

4. **Listen to the other side** and make small concessions that address their core concerns.

5. **Be prepared to argue.** Research similar products and cite those as examples. Quote prices from other vendors selling or buying the same product. If available, include facts that neither party can dispute. Don't reveal all of your arguments at once. Instead, use them as examples throughout the conversation.

6. **Be aggressive in your position.** State that you will buy today if the vendor can meet your price. If selling, have the papers ready for signature.

7. **Walk away if you aren't getting anywhere.** Leave your phone number in case the other party reconsiders.

How to Read the Stock Index

Every guy should have some money in the stock market and, at the very least, in a 401(k) program. If you have invested properly, over time you will earn a return on your investments that will lay the foundation for future wealth. If you aren't interested in or capable of managing your investments, hire a broker to do the heavy lifting. You can keep track of your portfolio by reading the newspaper or visiting financial Web sites. Here's how you can evaluate the performance of any given stock:

1. Locate the abbreviated name of the company or its New York Stock Exchange ticker symbol.

2. The "52 week Hi" and "52 week Lo" are the highest and lowest prices that stock has sold over the past year. This will give you an idea of the price fluctuation over a period of time.

3. The "Div" is the dividend the stock is paying out to shareholders projected for the

year based on last quarter's reporting. The "Yld" is the dividend divided by the closing price of the stock. This percentage offers a glimpse of the return on your investment; the higher, the better.

4. The "PE" is the ratio of the stock's price compared to the company's earnings. This is a good ratio to use when comparing stocks because it factors in the actual success of the company in the marketplace.

5. "Vol" lists the number of trades executed on that stock the previous day. This gives you a good idea about the demand for that stock.

6. The "daily Hi" and "daily Lo" are the highest and lowest price that stock has sold for during that day.

7. "Close" and "Net Chg" indicate the price of the stock when the market closed and how that compares to the day before. This number gives you a good idea of which direction the stock is moving.

How to Give a Toast

You may be asked to give a toast at a wedding, a retirement party, or a birthday celebration. Use these tips to make the most of the occasion.

1. **Stay sober.** We know you're nervous, but you can drink when it's over.

2. **Keep it short, sweet, and sincere.** Don't force jokes—especially at the expense of the honoree(s). Include several compliments.

3. **Make it personal.** Address the honoree(s) by name. Include your relationship and a few memorable stories or accomplishments.

4. **Own the speech.** Commit the toast to memory, if possible. Speak slowly, clearly, and confidently.

5. **Make a connection with the honoree(s) and the other attendees.** Look people in the eye and raise your glass.

How to Make a Great First Impression

You only get one chance to make a first impression. Whether you're meeting your girlfriend's family or a potential client, get it right the first time with these tips.

1. **Look the part.** Dress properly for the setting. When in doubt, overdress.

2. **Greet the person(s) with a firm handshake.** Make eye contact. You can never go wrong with a timeless remark such as, "It's a pleasure to meet you."

3. **Speak carefully and clearly.** Employ a moderate pace that allows you to enunciate. Use proper grammar.

4. **Be polite and courteous** in your tone. Avoid jokes until you are very comfortable with the situation and certain that the joke will be met with the proper response.

5. **Address the person properly** and use their name frequently. In order to do so, it is im-

portant to memorize their name upon first introduction.

6. **Focus the conversation on the other person.** Ask questions to learn more about them and to keep the dialogue moving forward.

7. **Listen carefully.** Don't hesitate to use verbal cues ("I understand") and visual cues (nodding your head in agreement) to indicate that you are paying close attention.

How to Give a Good Compliment

Whether you're speaking to a beautiful woman you've just met or chatting with the old man who manages the office mail room, it always pays to be nice. If this skill doesn't come naturally, follow these simple guidelines.

1. **Be observant and specific.** Your attention to detail will make the compliment more meaningful. Example: "I admire your respect for the environment."

2. **Justify the compliment.** Your reason for giving the compliment will reinforce its sincerity. Example: "I admire your respect for the environment and the way you're taking steps to improve it."

3. **Use an example.** Cement your sincerity by recounting a story. Example: "I admire your respect for the environment and the way you're taking steps to improve it. It was really great how you set up the recycling program at our office."

4. **Ask a question.** This can also act as a conversation starter. Example: "I admire your respect for the environment and the way you're taking steps to improve it. It was really great how you set up the recycling program at our office. Is there anything I can do to help?"

5. **Follow up later.** A thoughtful e-mail or thank-you note is always appreciated. There's no need to be wordy. It's the thought that counts. Example: "Thank you so much for taking the time to show us how to sort our office recyclables. Your dedication to this project has been inspirational."

Five Pick-Up Lines in Five Different Languages

English	French	Spanish
"What do people do for fun around here?"	"Qu'est-ce qu'on fait pour s'éclater ici?"	"Que hace la gente aqui para divertirse?"
"Do you come here often?"	"Tu viens souvent ici?"	"Vienes aqui a menudo?"
"May I have the pleasure of this dance?"	"Voulez-vous m'accorder cette danse?"	"Puerdo tener el honor de este baile?"
"Can I buy you a drink?"	"Je peux t'offrir un verre?"	"Puedo invitarte a un trago?"
"You have beautiful eyes."	"T'as de beaux yeux, tu sais."	"Tienes unos ojos muy bonitos."

German	Italian
"Was macht man hier, wenn man einen draufmachen will?"	"Cosa si fa qui per divertirsi?"
"Kommst du oft hier?"	"Vieni qua spesso?"
"Darf ich um diesen Tanz bitten?"	"Posso avere l'onore di questo ballo?"
"Kann ich dich zum Drink einladen?"	"Posso offrirti da bere?"
"Du hast wunderschöne Augen."	"Che occhi belli che hai."

How to Pick Up a Woman

Don't think of parties and bars as the only places where you stand a chance of picking up a woman. In fact, you might have better chances if you gather up the nerve to pick up a pretty woman you meet in your neighborhood, on the subway, or at the park.

1. **Stay calm and confident.** What do you have to lose?

2. **Ask her about herself:** her job, her family, her dog, or how her day is going. Show her that you are interested in more than just her looks. Resist the urge to boast. She'll be more impressed if you display an ability to listen and make good conversation.

3. **Introduce yourself.** And make sure that you've gotten her name right. If you have trouble with names, connect her name to a word or image that reminds you of her.

4. **Maintain eye contact.** Exude confidence and poise. If her body language is similar to yours, chances are she's interested.

5. **Don't get uptight.** If you find yourself saying something corny, have the good nature to laugh at yourself and the situation.

6. **Ask for her number** and suggest that the two of you get together within the next week or even that very moment. If you suggest plans in person, you'll have something to talk about when you call her later.

7. **Don't be afraid to call her,** but resist the urge to call or text her multiple times a day.

How to Last Ten Minutes on the Dance Floor

If you attend a wedding reception but refuse to dance, you're being a bad guest. No one's expecting you to move like Fred Astaire. You just need to stick to the basics.

Slow dancing:

1. Face your partner.

2. Place both hands on the small of her back. Or place your dominant hand on the small of her back and your other hand stretched away from your body holding her hand.

3. Slide from side to side while taking slight steps forward to move in a clockwise motion. Ideally, your footwork is a mirror image of hers, and your left foot moves to your left as her right foot moves to her right.

4. Use your dominant hand to guide your partner in the direction you want her to move.

5. Maintain eye contact with your partner. At first, you may need to watch your feet

to get a handle on her dance style. But ultimately, you should look straight ahead.

6. Compliment her dancing or make smalltalk.

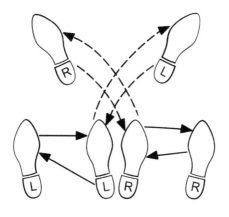

Fast dancing:

Each fast song has a different beat. Identify that beat and move in time with it.

1. Soak in the atmosphere. Get a feel for the type of music that is being played and how others are dancing.

2. Listen to the music and find the beat. Bounce your body to get the rhythm.

3. When you're ready, find a place on the dance floor. Circle up if there's a group. Or face your partner.

4. Start with your feet together. Move your right foot to the side and bring it back in. Keep going. Mix it up by stepping forward, backward, and diagonally.

5. Move your arms to the beat. Don't flail them around, but don't keep them stiff either.

6. Face forward and try to make it look effortless. You don't want to concentrate too hard.

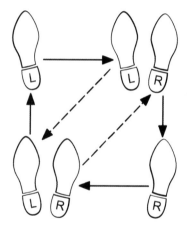

Fast Dancing

Tips for the Grill

Guys and grills go together like love and marriage. And once you're married, this is one of the few places in the world where your wife will leave you alone. Make the most of your grilling with these simple tips:

- **Chicken:** Marinate chicken overnight to allow the flavor to sink in. Also, white meat cooks faster than dark meat, so plan your timing accordingly.

- **Steak:** When steak is finished cooking, remove it from the grill and let it sit for a few minutes to allow the juices to redistribute through the steak.

- **Burgers:** Flip your burgers only once. This will give them great char marks and keep the juices sealed inside.

- **Fish:** Use a fish basket to keep the fish from sticking to the grill. It will also prevent the top layer from flaking off and releasing some of the flavor.

- **Ribs:** Reduce your grill time by boiling ribs ahead of time.

How to Make the Perfect Omelet

If you want to really impress a woman, try impressing her in the kitchen. After all, you gotta eat.

1. Crack two eggs in a bowl. Add a splash of milk and a sprinkle of black pepper. Mix with a fork until smooth.

2. Coat a small pan with cooking spray or butter and place over a medium flame. Let the pan heat for a few moments.

3. Pour in the egg mixture so that it evenly fills the pan. Let it set for 30 seconds.

4. Use a spatula to lift the edges of the egg mixture so that the uncooked eggs can move to the bottom.

5. Once the egg mixture is almost cooked, add some fillings to one half of the pan. Fillings can include diced tomatoes, ham, bacon, spinach, broccoli, mushrooms, smoked salmon, onions, chives, spices, sauces, and virtually anything else you'd like

to include (see suggestions, opposite). The only requirement, typically, is some kind of shredded cheese. Do not overfill.

6. Use a spatula to fold the empty half of the egg mixture onto the filling; the result will have the shape of a half-moon.

7. Let the omelet cook for another 30 seconds.

8. Slide your spatula under the omelet and transport it to a plate.

Classic Omelet Fillings

Alaskan omelet: salmon, sour cream, chopped tarragon

Denver omelet: ham, green peppers, onion, cheddar cheese

French/Western omelet: ham, tomatoes, mushrooms

Greek omelet: spinach, black olives, feta cheese

Hawaiian omelet: ham, pineapple chunks, cheddar cheese, Monterey jack cheese

Irish omelet: mashed potato, lemon juice, chives

Polish omelet: potatoes, onion, zucchini

Seafood omelet: crab meat, shrimp, onions, mushrooms, sour cream, Swiss cheese

Spanish omelet: sliced potato, onions, red and green peppers

Southwest omelet: ham, tomato, green peppers or chilies, onions, salsa

Tips for Taking a Great Photograph

She'll want to cherish the moment forever. Maybe you will, too. Don't blow it with a blurry or overexposed shot.

1. Read the instruction manual that comes with your camera. Familiarize yourself with all of its features. Most contemporary digital cameras will do a lot of the work—including lighting and focusing—automatically.

2. To assist in composition, visualize a tic-tac-toe grid over the image in your viewfinder. Then place your subject near one of the corners of the center square. Placing the subject a bit off-center creates a more interesting photograph.

3. Watch your background. Wait for bystanders to get out of the way. Be certain there are no trees or skyscrapers "sticking out" of your subject's head.

4. Check your lighting. If you are outdoors, avoid direct lighting, which may cause squinting and shadows. Also, unless you're photographing a sunset, it's generally better to stand with your back to the sun. If you are indoors, consider turning on more lights or moving lights closer to your subject.

5. Try unique angles. They may bring a whole new perspective to your photograph.

6. Although more difficult to get right, an action shot or candid offers a more realistic shot since the facial expressions will not seem as forced. To ensure good candids, practice by taking lots and lots (and lots) of photographs. Remember, on a digital camera, you can always delete the bad ones.

How to Give a Great Massage

A massage is a great way to bring two people together in an intimate moment. When done properly, it relieves stress and channels positive energy—and can also lead to a more sensual experience.

1. Set the mood. Eliminate all outside distractions, such as pets and children. Dim the lights. Draw the curtains. Set the room to a comfortable temperature. Play calm and relaxing music.

2. Have your partner disrobe as much as she feels comfortable. It's possible to give a good massage over clothing, but it's not ideal. Depending on your relationship, you might leave the room during this step.

3. Ask your partner to lie face down on a firm surface that supports her whole body.

4. You or your partner should drape a plain sheet over her body. During the massage, you will fold back the sheet when you wish

to massage a specific area and replace it when you move to another area.

5. Quality massage oil can be the difference between a good massage and a great one. Avoid cheap oils with synthetic scents and greasy textures. Warm the massage oil by rubbing it between your palms.

6. Employ the following basic strokes:

   a. **Effleurage:** Apply soft and fluid strokes firmly with the palm of your hand.

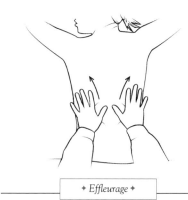

✦ Effleurage ✦

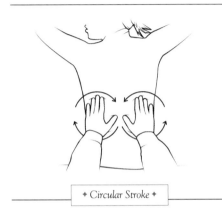

+ Circular Stroke +

b. Circular stroke: Apply pressure as you move your hand in a clockwise motion.

c. Kneading: Squeeze and release the flesh and muscle.

8. Begin with her shoulders. Make smooth and soft strokes using your entire hand. Pull the stress away from her core and out of her body.

9. Gently work down to her back. Remember

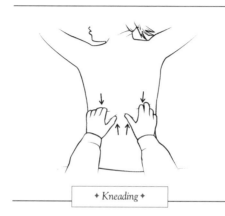

✦ *Kneading* ✦

that you are not a licensed chiropractor.

10. Work on her arms, hands, and fingers, then move to her legs, feet, and toes. Finish with a scalp rub using only your finger tips.

12. Use a soft towel to wipe the oil away.

Tip: Resist the urge to transform the massage into a sexual encounter. If your partner is looking for a happy ending, you'll be the first to know.

How to Buy Clothes for a Woman

Oh, this is risky. If you are going to do this, it is imperative that you do it right. Start by taking notice of what she chooses for herself. It will help you purchase something she will like.

1. Observe her style. It is typical for a woman to mix styles in her wardrobe and even in the same outfit.

    a. Casual styles include a comfortable and sporty influence, such as denim.

    b. Classic styles are more polished and chic and may include a blazer.

    c. Contemporary styles include the latest fashion trends.

2. Find out where she likes to shop and which labels she wears. Although most stores carry a variety of labels and price points, some designers can be found only in proprietary shops. Do your research ahead of time.

3. You'll need to know her measurements. Take a look at the tags. In the U.S., there are four typical categories:

   a. Juniors: odd numbers 0–13

   b. Women's: even numbers 2–14

   c. Plus: 14 and up

   d. Petite: even numbers 0–14, cut to fit women less than 5'4" tall

4. Obviously, you want to select a flattering item. Consider these tips:

   a. Minimize the bells and whistles. Keep it simple.

   b. Dark colors are slimming. Unless you're a pro, avoid stripes of any kind.

   c. V-necks and turtlenecks call attention to her face.

5. Be sure to ask for a gift receipt (no matter how much you think she'll like it), and slip it into the gift wrap.

How to Buy a Diamond

If you plan on making a marriage proposal, you may be in the market for a diamond engagement ring. To ensure that your investment obtains the desired result, follow these tips.

- **Consider the color.** In the world of diamonds, color is graded on an alphabetical scale ranging from "colorless" (D) to "light yellow" (Z). You want the diamond you choose to have as little color as possible. Note that grades G, H, I, and J are considered "near colorless" and offer an incredible value (these stones only appear to have color when compared to other diamonds).

- **Consider the cut.** This refers to the general way a diamond is cut into facets and determines the way light travels through the stone, which affects its brilliance. Cut isn't really measured in any unit, but you want to avoid a diamond that seems too squat/shallow or too deep.

- **Consider the carat.** This is the weight of a

diamond. It has the largest impact on the price. It will ultimately decide how visible the diamond is in the setting and on her finger.

- **Consider the clarity.** This measurement charts the flawlessness of a stone. Clarity is graded on a scale from "flawless" to "included," with varying stages of imperfections along the way. "Very slightly included" and "slightly included" are in the mid-range and considered a solid value.

- **Consider the shape.** Round and emerald-cut diamonds are more traditional, but there are many trendier options available. Ask your wife-to-be what she likes. Since you're getting married, you need to familiarize yourself with this question, anyway.

- **Check the authenticity.** Before purchasing, you are entitled to view the diamond's grading report certifying that it has been examined, scrutinized and graded by a team of gemologists. The report should list all of the diamond's key characteristics, as listed above.

How to Propose

If you plan on taking that next big step, you've got to do it right. Here are some basic tips for popping the question.

1. **Think it through.** Is this the woman you want to spend the rest of your life with? Are you fairly confident that she feels the same way? If you have any doubts, you may want to wait another year before popping the question.

2. **Buy a ring.** No matter how big or small, an engagement ring will let her know that you're serious about this commitment. (See page 136 for tips on buying a diamond.) Make sure to keep the ring (either in or out of the box) in a safe, yet easily accessible place, such as the pocket of your blazer.

3. **Pick a location.** Plan a special romantic evening based on your soon-to-be fiancée's tastes. If she gets easily embarrassed, do not propose in a crowded restaurant or on the

JumboTron at a sports stadium. Choose a place that is meaningful for both of you.

4. **Express your feelings.** On the big night, tell her how much you love her and how much she means to you. Make eye contact, and don't rush your words. Savor the moment you'll both remember forever.

4. **Kneel.** Some women may not appreciate such a chivalrous gesture, but many consider it essential. The decision rests with you.

5. **Offer her the ring.** When you give her the ring, hold it toward the light to make it sparkle. Wait until she has accepted your proposal to put it on her ring finger.

6. **Ask her to marry you.** Always introduce the idea of marriage in the form of a question. That way there is no confusion, and her choice of answers is fairly simple. Wait for her to answer before continuing with the evening. Good luck.

Wedding Anniversary Chart

Most guys can remember their wedding anniversary. But can they remember the appropriate gift for each milestone? When in doubt, consult this chart. And always add flowers.

Year	Gift	Gem
1	Paper	Gold Jewelry
2	Cotton	Garnet
3	Leather	Pearls
4	Linen	Blue Topaz
5	Wood	Sapphire
10	Tin	Diamond
15	Crystal	Ruby
25	Silver	Silver Jubilee
50	Gold	Golden Jubilee

Simple Answers to Difficult Questions

Every romantic relationship brings its share of tough questions. To ensure domestic harmony, keep these replies handy and never deviate from the script.

Question	Suggested Response
"Do you love me?"	"Yes."
"How much do you love me?"	"More and more with each passing day."
"Do you think that girl was pretty?"	"What girl?"
"Who was the best lover you've ever had?"	"You."
"Seriously?"	"Kiss me."

"What are you thinking about?"	"All the ways we can spend the day together."
"Does this blouse/ skirt/dress make me look fat?"	"Are you kidding? I've never seen you look more beautiful."
"Who would you marry if I died?"	"I can't imagine ever being attracted to anyone else."

Stuff You Should Know But I Can't Tell You

1. Birthdays and anniversaries for your spouse/girlfriend, all close family members, friends, and key coworkers

2. How to escape your house during a fire

3. The best bar and restaurant in your neighborhood for visiting out-of-towners

4. Your signature cocktail, so you're never dumbfounded when called upon

5. Your shirt size, pant size, and jacket size

6. Your signature dish, so you're always prepared to impress a date/your spouse

7. Your favorite book, movie, and band

8. Your spouse's/girlfriend's favorite book, movie, and band

9. Your family history, so that you can tell it to your children someday

10. What you want out of life

How to Say Thank You

1. Keep it short and simple.

Thanks to Jason Rekulak for encouraging me to step up and write this book and helping me put it together. Thanks to everyone at Quirk Books for making this book and all of our books the best products on the planet.

Thanks to my family: Randi, Ilivia, "Mc-Nabb," and Dylan; Phil and Sheryl; Harvey and Rosalie; Mandi, Adam, and Lexi; Brett, Shawn, Andrew, Ashley, and Hailey; Brian and Pamela; and Gladys and Lena.

Thanks to my friends: Adam, Jeff, Matt, and Seth; and FND, Fantan, and SOHK.